Investigative

Developing children's investigative and thinking skills in the Daily Maths Lesson

Year
4

Peter Clarke

William Collins' dream of knowledge for all began with the publication of his first book in 1819. A self-educated mill worker, he not only enriched millions of lives, but also founded a flourishing publishing house. Today, staying true to this spirit, Collins books are packed with inspiration, innovation and practical expertise. They place you at the centre of a world of possibility and give you exactly what you need to explore it.

Collins. Do more.

Published by Collins
An imprint of HarperCollins*Publishers*
77–85 Fulham Palace Road
Hammersmith
London
W6 8JB

Browse the complete Collins catalogue at
www.collinseducation.com

10 9 8 7 6 5 4 3 2 1

ISBN 0 00 719474 9

Peter Clarke asserts his moral right to be identified as the author of this work

British Library Cataloguing in Publication Data
A Catalogue record for this publication is available from the British Library

Publishing Manager: Melanie Hoffman
Project Editor: Natasha Reid
Editor: Jean Rustean
Cover design by Susi Martin
Cover illustration by Gary Dunn
Series design by Neil Adams
Illustrations by Juliet Breese

Printed and bound by Martins the Printers, Berwick on Tweed

Contents

Introduction

Mathematical problem solving encompasses both using and applying mathematics to the solution of problems arising from the environment and reasoning and investigating questions that have arisen from within mathematics itself.

Being able to use mathematics to analyse situations and solve real-life problems is a major reason for studying the subject. Frequent use of everyday experiences will give meaning to the children's mathematical experiences. Children need to be able to apply the mathematics they have learned to real-life situations in their environment. They also need to be able to interpret and make meaning from their results. Teachers should structure situations in which children investigate problems relevant to their daily lives and relating to the recent mathematical knowledge, skills and understanding the children have acquired.

Studies of effective teachers of numeracy (Askew *et al.* 1997) have found that the most effective teachers have a 'connectionist' orientation to the teaching of mathematics. These teachers encourage children to think and talk about what they are doing and to make connections between different areas and aspects of the subject.

Investigative Maths is a series of six books for Year 1 to Year 6. It is designed to assist children to practise and consolidate the three strands of the Mathematics National Curriculum Attainment Target 1 – Using and applying mathematics: problem solving, communicating and reasoning; as well as the problem solving strand of the National Numeracy Strategy (NNS) *Framework for teaching mathematics R – 6*. At the same time other key mathematical strands are also developed such as numbers and the number system, calculations, and measures, shape and space.

Investigative Maths aims to provide teachers with a resource that enables children to:

- use and apply mathematics to solve problems arising from the environment
- reason and investigate questions that have arisen from within mathematics itself
- practise their pure mathematical knowledge and skills in an applied context
- apply their mathematical problem solving skills in contexts that are topical, relevant and meaningful

The activities

Investigative Maths contains two different types of activities:

Everyday problem solving

These activities include problems arising from the environment.

The activities in this section have been organised into themes. There are 12 themes, each with four different activities. The four activities can either be used together in one lesson, with different groups working on different activities, or individually over the course of a week or more.

When children solve everyday problems:

- the purpose and meaning is clear
- it is motivating

- it allows them to take control of the mathematics, choosing methods that suit them
- they are likely to feel confident about multi-tasking
- the context provides many clues and stimuli to support their thinking
- the mathematics is practical rather than abstract, and builds more obviously on children's previous experiences

Mathematical problem solving

These activities include problems arising from within mathematics itself.

When children solve mathematical problems they:

- use prior mathematical knowledge to acquire new mathematical knowledge
- make connections

Resources

- Almost all the activities in *Investigative Maths* suggest that pencil and paper be given to the children. This allows the children to feel free to work out the answers and record their thinking in ways that are appropriate to them. Giving children a large sheet of paper, such as A1, provides them with an excellent prompt to use when discussing their work, especially during the plenary. It also aids assessment for children's problem solving, communicating and reasoning skills.
- An important problem solving skill is to be able to identify not only the mathematics, but also what equipment to use. For this reason many of the activities do not name the specific resources that are needed. For example, in problems involving measures, the resources section states simply 'measuring equipment' to make teachers aware that a range of measuring equipment will need to be on hand for the children to choose.
- Teachers also need to be aware that some of the activities require them or the children to bring in to school resources from home.

Answers

- In the *Mathematical problem solving* section, answers are given to the primary activities where necessary, not to the extensions .
- In the *Everyday problem solving* section, no answers are given.

Investigative Maths and the daily mathematics lesson

The activities contained in *Investigative Maths* are ideally suited to the daily mathematics lesson. They can be used to:

- introduce new mathematical concepts using a discovery approach to teaching and learning
- consolidate children's understanding of previously taught mathematical concepts
- provide an opportunity for children to use and apply their 'pure' mathematical knowledge in more applied, problem solving and investigative contexts
- extend the more able pupils
- challenge the 'quick finishers'

Although the activities are designed to be used by individuals, pairs or groups of children, they will be enhanced greatly if children are able to work together in pairs or groups. By working collaboratively, children are more likely to develop their problem solving, communicating and reasoning skills.

Problem solving skills

Investigative Maths aims to develop in children the key skills required to tackle and solve mathematical investigations.

These include:
- reading and making sense of a problem
- recognising key words, relevant information and redundant information
- finding parts of a problem that can be tackled
- recognising the mathematics which can be used to help solve a problem
- deciding which number operation(s) to perform and in which order
- choosing an efficient way of calculating
- presenting information and results in a clear and organised way
- changing measurements to the same units before calculating
- getting into the habit of checking for themselves whether the answer makes sense

Thinking skills

The National Curriculum (2000) outlines the thinking skills that complement the key knowledge, skills and understanding which are embedded in the primary curriculum.

Investigative Maths aims to develop in children these key thinking skills.

Information – processing skills
- locate, collect relevant information
- sort, classify, sequence, compare and analyse part and/or whole relationships

Reasoning skills
- give reasons for opinions and actions
- draw inferences and make deductions
- use precise language to explain what they think
- make judgements and decisions informed by reason or evidence

Enquiry skills
- ask relevant questions
- pose and define problems
- plan what to do and how to research
- predict outcomes and anticipate conclusions
- test conclusions and improve ideas

Creative thinking skills
- generate and extend ideas
- suggest hypotheses
- apply imagination
- look for alternative innovative outcomes

Evaluative skills
- evaluate information
- judge the value of what they read, hear or do
- develop criteria for judging the value of their own and others' work or ideas
- have confidence in their judgement

Problem solving strategies

If children are actively to engage in mathematical investigations they must be taught appropriate problem solving strategies.

Children need to be taught to:
- look for a pattern or sequence
- experiment or act out a problem
- make a drawing or model
- make a list, table or chart
- write a number sentence
- see mathematical connections
- make and test a prediction
- make a generalisation
- establish a proof
- account for all known possibilities
- solve a simpler related problem
- work backwards

A model for mathematical investigations

To be successful at solving mathematical investigations, children need to:
- be given ample opportunities to practise problem solving skills and strategies
- work systematically and co-operatively
- use what knowledge and skills they have to help acquire new knowledge and skills
- develop self monitoring and self assessment
- talk about their work and reflect on their thinking

The model on page 8 provides children with a systematic approach to solving mathematical investigations. It also enables children to practise and develop their thinking skills.

Photocopy and enlarge this page, make it into a poster, and display it for all the class to see and follow.

Children need to be taught to use this model flexibly. They must realise that:
- not all eight stages of the model are required for every investigation
- the amount of time that is spent on each of the eight stages depends upon the nature of the investigation
- any stage in the model can be revisited at any time

A model for mathematical investigations

Recognise
What is the problem?

Reflect
What have I learned from this?

Use
What do I already know that can help me solve this problem?

Share
Let's tell others.

Support
What do I need to find out and use to help me solve this problem?

Check and assess
- Am I correct?
- How well did I do?

Decide and try
- How might I go about solving this problem?
- What is the best way?
- Let's try.

Review
Is it working?
Yes – Let's continue.
No – Let's go back.

Investigative Maths (Y4) © HarperCollins*Publishers* Ltd 2005

Curriculum information

The activities in *Investigative Maths* are designed to improve children's attainment in the three strands of the National Curriculum Attainment Target 1 – Using and applying mathematics.

In *problem solving* by:

- using a range of problem solving strategies
- trying different approaches to a problem
- applying mathematics in a new context
- checking their results

In *communicating* by:

- interpreting information
- recording information systematically
- using mathematical language, symbols, notation and diagrams correctly and precisely
- presenting and interpreting methods, solutions and conclusions in the context of the problem

In *reasoning* by:

- giving clear explanations of their methods and reasoning
- investigating and making general statements
- recognising patterns in their results
- making use of a wider range of evidence to justify results through logical reasoned argument
- drawing their own conclusions

The activities also provide children with an opportunity to practise and consolidate the following Year 4 solving problems objectives from the NNS *Framework*:

Topic: *Making decisions*

- Choose and use appropriate number operations and appropriate ways of calculating (mental, mental with jottings, pencil and paper) to solve problems.

Topic: *Reasoning about numbers or shapes*

- Explain methods and reasoning about numbers orally and in writing.
- Solve mathematical problems or puzzles, recognise and explain patterns and relationships, generalise and predict. Suggest extensions by asking 'What if…?'
- Make and investigate a general statement about familiar numbers or shapes by finding examples that satisfy it.

Topic: *Problems involving 'real life', money or measures*

- Use all four operations to solve word problems involving numbers in 'real life', money and measures (including time), using one or more steps, including converting pounds to pence and metres to centimetres and vice versa.

In addition to these objectives, the charts on pages 10 and 11 show which other strand(s) and topic(s) each of the activities covers.

Everyday problem solving

These activities include problems arising from the environment.

Page	Activity	Theme	Title	Place value, ordering and rounding	Properties of numbers and number sequences	Fractions and decimals	Addition	Subtraction	Multiplication	Division	Money	Organising and using data	Measures: Length (L), Mass (M), Capacity (C), Time (T), Area (A), Perimeter (P)	Shape and space
14	1a	Number systems	Ancient Greek numbers	●	●							●		
14	1b		Roman numerals	●	●							●		
15	1c		Ancient Egyptian number symbols	●	●							●		
15	1d		Your own number system	●	●							●		
16	2a	Post	How much post?	●			●		●			●		
16	2b		Post boxes	●									● L	
17	2c		Postage weights					●			●		● M	
17	2d		How much to post?				●	●	●	●	●		● M	
18	3a	Diet and nutrition	Weight of food				●	●					● M	
18	3b		Calorific value	●				●	●	●				
19	3c		Balanced menu				●	●	●			●	● M	
19	3d		Packaged food			●						●		
20	4a	Timetables	Class timetable				●	●				●	● T	
20	4b		Cinema timetable									●	● T	
21	4c		Local timetables								●	●	● L,T	
21	4d		Your timetable									●	● T	
22	5a	Seaside	Seaside holiday									●	● L,T	
22	5b		Sandcastles										● M	
23	5c		Tides					●					● T	
23	5d		Symmetrical sea											●
24	6a	Home work	Jobs around the house									●	● T	
24	6b		Jobs worth				●		●		●	●	● T	
25	6c		Cooking				●	●	●	●	●	●	● M,C	
25	6d		Painting	●			●	●	●			●	● L,A	
26	7a	Streets	Street uses				●					●		
26	7b		Street map											●
27	7c		People in your street	●			●	●						
27	7d		Money trail					●			●		● L	
28	8a	Recycling	School recycling				●		●				● M	
28	8b		Home recycling				●		●		●		● M	
29	8c		Rubbish				●		●				● M	
29	8d		Second-hand stall				●					●		
30	9a	Cars	Popular cars									●		
30	9b		Family car	●			●		●		●		● L	
31	9c		Number plates				●	●	●	●				
31	9d		Travelling				●					●	● L,T	
32	10a	Holidays	Planning a holiday				●		●		●			
32	10b		Package holiday				●		●		●		● T	
33	10c		Visiting our local area									●	● T,L	
33	10d		School holidays			●	●	●	●	●			● T	
34	11a	Classroom	Newly designed classroom										● L	●
34	11b		Paper				●		●			●	● M	
35	11c		Windows	●					●				● A	
35	11d		How many children?	●			●		●				● A,P	
36	12a	Shopping	Shops in the local area									●		
36	12b		Biggest and busiest									●		
37	12c		Cost of the same item					●			●			
37	12d		Packaging											●

Mathematical problem solving

These activities include problems arising from within mathematics itself.

Page	Activity	Title	Strand: Numbers and the number system			Calculations				Solving problems		Measures, shape and space	
			Place value, ordering and rounding	Properties of numbers and number sequences	Fractions and decimals	Addition	Subtraction	Multiplication	Division	Money	Organising and using data	Measures: Length (L), Mass (M), Capacity (C), Time (T), Area (A), Perimeter (P)	Shape and space
38	13	Making numbers	●								●		
38	14	Ordering numbers	●	●							●		
39	15	Nearest 10 and 100	●										
39	16	Divisible by 4		●				●	●				
40	17	Multiples of 10 between …		●									
40	18	Number sequences	●	●							●		
41	19	Common multiples		●							●		
41	20	Rolling fractions			●								
42	21	Fractions of amounts			●			●	●		●		
42	22	Fraction families			●				●				
43	23	Making decimals			●						●		
43	24	2 numbers totalling 100				●					●		
44	25	Consecutive decimals			●	●							
44	26	Addition and subtraction cards				●	●				●		
45	27	Totals and differences	●			●	●				●		
45	28	Dice calculations	●			●	●				●		
46	29	3-card calculations	●			●	●						
46	30	Making predictions	●	●		●	●				●		
47	31	Consecutive reversals				●	●				●		
47	32	Reversing palindromic numbers				●	●				●		
48	33	Telephone totals				●	●						
48	34	Using tables						●					
49	35	Multiplying by 19 and 21						●					
49	36	2-digit × 1-digit				●		●					
50	37	Division cards							●		●		
50	38	Dividing by 7		●					●				
51	39	9							●				
51	40	Many multiplications						●	●		●		
52	41	Broken calculator				●	●	●					
52	42	True statements	●			●	●	●	●				
53	43	1, 10, 100 and 1000	●		●	●	●	●	●				
53	44	Amazing function machines	●			●		●					
54	45	Domino calculations				●	●	●	●				
54	46	£3 please!				●				●	●		
55	47	Paying bills				●	●			●	●		
55	48	Calculating with pence			●	●	●			●			
56	49	Pounds and pence			●	●	●			●			
56	50	Spirals	●									●L	
57	51	Shopping basket				●						●M	
57	52	Making fruit juice			●	●		●	●			●C	
58	53	Light bars										●T	
58	54	Area and perimeter				●		●				●A,P	
59	55	Different areas and perimeters				●		●				●A,P	
59	56	Pentominoes									●		●
60	57	Symmetrical shapes											●
60	58	Shortest route											●
61	59	Right angles?											●
61	60	Angle times											●

Assessment and record keeping

Investigative Maths activities may be used with the whole class or with groups of children as an assessment activity. Linked to the topic that is being studied at present, *Investigative Maths* will provide you with an indication of how well the children have understood the objectives being covered as well as their problem solving skills.

The Assessment and record keeping format on page 13 can be used to assess and level children in Attainment Target 1: Using and applying mathematics. By observing individual children while they undertake an *Investigative Maths* activity, discussing their work with them, and subsequently marking their work, you will be able to gain a good understanding of their problem solving, communicating and reasoning skills.

Your judgements about an individual child's abilities should also take into account:

- mastery of other objectives from the 'Solving problems' strand of the NNS *Framework*
- performance in whole class discussions
- participation in group work
- work presented in exercise books
- any other written evidence

Once you have decided which level 'best fits' a particular child write the child's name in the box under the appropriate level. You may wish to identify how competent a child is at that level by using the following key:

C – Becoming competent in most criteria at this level

B – Competent in most criteria at this level

A – Very competent in most criteria at this level

It is envisaged that one copy of the Assessment and record keeping format would be used for your entire class.

Attainment Target 1: Using and applying mathematics

Assessment and record keeping format

Year: _____   Class: _____

Teacher: _____

LEVEL 2

Problem solving
- Select and use material in some classroom activities.
- Select and use mathematics for some classroom activities.
- Begin to develop own strategies for solving a problem.
- Begin to understand ways of working through a problem.

Communicating
- Discuss work using mathematical language.
- Respond to and ask mathematical questions.
- Begin to represent work using symbols and simple diagrams.
- Explain why an answer is correct.

Reasoning
- Ask questions such as: 'What would happen if...?' 'Why?'.
- Begin to develop simple strategies.

LEVEL 3

Problem solving
- Develop different mathematical approaches to a problem.
- Look for ways to overcome difficulties.
- Begin to make decisions and realise that results may vary according to the 'rule' used.
- Begin to organise work.
- Check results.

Communicating
- Discuss mathematical work.
- Begin to explain thinking.
- Use and interpret mathematical symbols and diagrams.

Reasoning
- Understand a general statement.
- Investigate general statements and predictions by finding and trying out examples.

LEVEL 4

Problem solving
- Develop own strategies for solving problems.
- Use own strategies for working within mathematics.
- Use own strategies for applying mathematics to practical contexts.

Communicating
- Present information and results in a clear and organised way.

Reasoning
- Search for solutions by trying out own ideas.

GENERAL COMMENTS

1a

Ancient Greek numbers

- pencil and paper

Ancient Greeks did not use the digits 1–9 as we do today. Instead, the letters of their alphabet were used with a ' or , to represent numbers.

α'	β'	γ'	δ'	ε'	ς'	ζ'	η'	θ'
1	2	3	4	5	6	7	8	9
ι'	κ'	λ'	μ'	ν'	ξ'	ο'	π'	φ'
10	20	30	40	50	60	70	80	90
ρ'	σ'	τ'	υ'	φ'	χ'	ψ'	ω'	⊐
100	200	300	400	500	600	700	800	900
,α	,β	,γ	,δ	,ε	,ς	,ζ	,η	,θ
1000	2000	3000	4000	5000	6000	7000	8000	9000

$31 = λα'$ $752 = ψνβ'$ $8193 = ,ηρφγ$

- Use the Ancient Greek alphabet to write the following dates:
  - 776 BC (The year of the first Ancient Olympic Games.)
  - 395 AD (The year of the last Ancient Olympic Games.)
  - 1896 AD (The year of the first Modern Olympic Games.)

- Choose 10 different 2-digit numbers and write them using Ancient Greek numbers.
- What about choosing 10 different 3-digit and 4-digit numbers?

1b

Roman numerals

- pencil and paper

Roman numerals was the standard numbering system in Ancient Rome and Europe until about 900 AD.

I	II	III	IV	V	VI	VII	VIII	IX	X	L	C	D	M
1	2	3	4	5	6	7	8	9	10	50	100	500	1000

37 = XXXVII   892 = DCCCXCII   1448 = MCDXLVIII

- Use Roman numerals to write:
  - 43 AD (The year the Romans invaded Britain.)
  - 122 AD (The year Hadrian's Wall was started.)
  - 410 AD (The year the Romans left Britain.)

- Choose 10 different 2-digit numbers and write them using Roman numerals.
- What about choosing 10 different 3-digit and 4-digit numbers?

1c Ancient Egyptian number symbols

• pencil and paper

The Ancient Egyptians had a number system using seven different symbols.

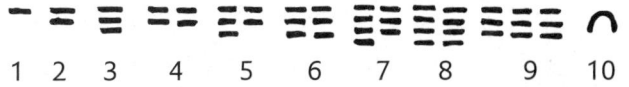

1	2	3	4	5	6	7	8	9	10

100	1000	10 000	100 000	1 000 000

= 3246

= 32 423

• Use the Ancient Egyptian number symbols to write:
  – 2560 BC (The year the Great Pyramid at Giza was built.)
  – 1343 BC (The year of Tutankhamun's death.)
  – 69 BC (The year of Cleopatra's birth.)

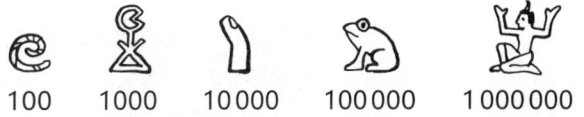

• Choose 10 different 2-digit numbers and write them using the Ancient Egyptian number symbols.

• What about choosing 10 different 3-digit and 4-digit numbers?

1d Your own number system

• pencil and paper

• Invent your own number system.

• Write or draw a description of your number system.

• Use your number system to write:
  – today's date
  – your birthday
  – another date you know.
    (Give it to a friend to decode.)

• Choose 10 different 2-digit numbers and write them using your number system.

• What about choosing 10 different 3-digit and 4-digit numbers?

2a How much post?

- pencil and paper

- How many letters and parcels are posted from your school each day?
- How many letters and parcels are received by your school each day?
- What proportion of the mail is:
  - letters
  - parcels
  - first class
  - second class
  - local
  - overseas.

- How do the results from your school compare with the number of letters that are posted and received in your house in a day?
- What about if you investigate this over a week / month / term / year?

2b Post boxes

- measuring equipment
- pencil and paper

- How many post boxes are in your area? How far apart are they?
- Approximately how far do you have to travel to post a letter?
- How far do most people in your area have to travel to post a letter?

- How are you going to measure the approximate distances people have to travel to post a letter?

2c Postage weights

- Looking at the stamps on the envelopes and using the Post Office Price Guide, work out the maximum that each envelope and its contents could have weighed.

This envelope and its contents must have weighed less than 34 g.

- Now weigh each envelope. Work out the maximum that the contents of each envelope could have weighed.

The maximum that the contents of this envelope could have weighed is 29 g.

- Post Office Price Guide
- collection of used, empty envelopes (not overseas) of varying sizes showing different values of stamps
- measuring equipment
- pencil and paper

2d How much to post?

- How much would it cost to send the following items to someone who lives in the same town as you?

- Post Office Price Guide
- collection of different sized envelopes
- magazine
- book
- sheets of paper
- set of photos
- measuring equipment
- pencil

magazine

book

letter

letter with photos

- Investigate the cost of sending other items.
- What if you sent these items to someone in a different country?

3a Weight of food

- measuring equipment
- pencil and paper

- Investigate the total weight of all the food you eat in a day.
- What about for a week?

- How does this compare to your weight?
- Compare the total weight of the food that you eat with the amount someone at home eats. Write about what you notice.

3b Calorific value

- pencil and paper

- What are calories?
- Approximately how many calories a day should you eat?
- Estimate the calorific value of what you ate yesterday.
- How does this compare with the amount of calories you should eat in a day?

- What about an adult in your home?
- Is the amount different for men and women?

3c Balanced menu

- food packaging
- pencil and paper

- Design a nutritious and balanced menu for a main meal.
- How much of each food will you need to feed a family of four?
- How much would it cost?
- Now design an unhealthy, unbalanced menu for a main meal.
- How much of each food will you need for a family of four?
- How much would this cost?
- Which meal is cheaper?

- Think about the portion sizes you are going to give everyone.

3d Packaged food

- different types of food packaging
- pencil and paper

- Investigate the Nutrition Information on different types of food packaging.
- Classify each food item into one of two groups: Healthy Food and Unhealthy Food.
- Explain why you classify each type of food the way you do.

- Think about:
  - how much fat each food contains
  - the amount of sugar they each contain
  - how many calories each food contains.

4a Class timetable

- class timetable
- pencil and paper

MONDAY	TUESDAY	WEDNESDAY	THURSDAY	FRIDAY
English	English	Assembly	Maths	Maths
Maths	Maths	English	English	English
Break				
Science	PE	Maths	Science	ICT
Lunch				
Art	Geography / History	PE	Geography / History	Design & Technology
		Music		

- How many hours a week do you spend on each subject?
- What fraction of the total time you spend in class do you spend on each subject?

- If you were your teacher, what changes would you make to your timetable? Why would you make these changes? Be prepared to justify your reasons.

4b Cinema timetable

- newspaper containing cinema timings
- pencil and paper

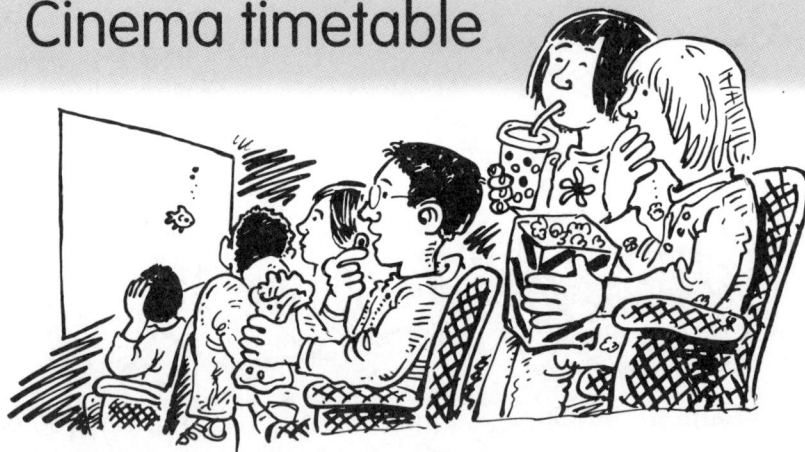

- Draw a daily timetable showing the starting and finishing times for each of the films at a local cinema.
- Now draw a weekly timetable.

- Think about:
  - on what day the cinema changes its programme
  - on what day of the week you are going to start your timetable.
- Make sure your timetable is as easy to read as possible.

4c Local timetables

- local bus or train timetable
- pencil and paper

- Look at a local bus or train timetable.
- Investigate how long it takes to travel between different places.
- Try and find out how much it costs.

- How long does the longest journey take?
- How long does the shortest journey take?

4d Your timetable

- pencil and paper

- Design a timetable of how you spend a week during term time.
- Include what you do at school and at home.

- Don't forget to include the time you spend eating, sleeping, watching TV, playing…

5a Seaside holiday

- sand and paper (pencil and paper)

- pencil and paper

- Choose a place by the seaside for you and your family to visit.
- How are you going to get there?
- How far away is it?
- How long will it take to travel there?
- Investigate how much it will cost to have a holiday at the seaside for your family for a week.

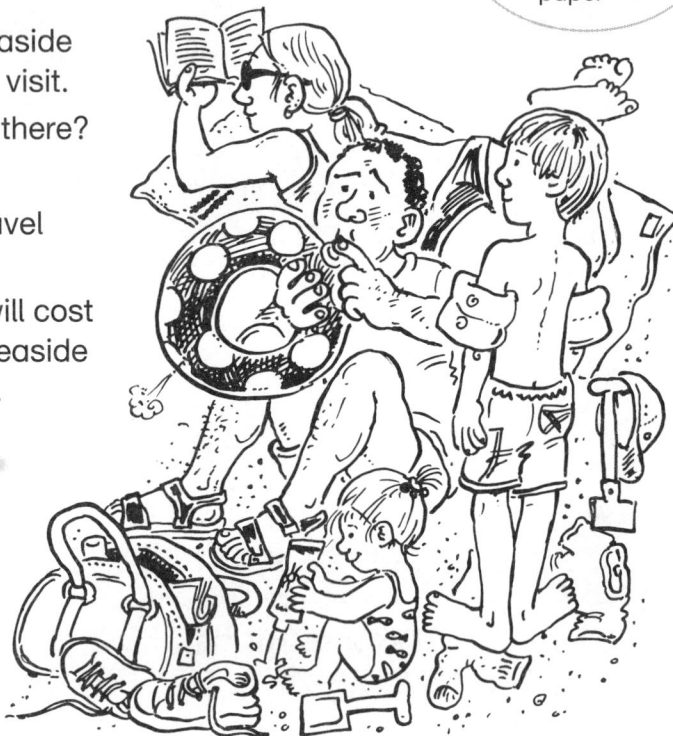

- Think about:
  - accommodation
  - travel costs
  - food
  - other expenses.

5b Sandcastles

- sand
- water
- various containers
- pencil and paper

- Build a sandcastle.
- Investigate how much it weighs.

- Think about how much a bucket of sand weighs.

5c Tides

Times and depths of high water 4–11 November				
Day	Morning	Height (m)	Evening	Height (m)
Thurs	08.38	6.8	21.18	6.8
Fri	09.38	7	22.18	
Sat	11.10	7.2		

- weather section from newspaper showing tides
- pencil and paper

- Look up the information about tides in the newspaper.
- Choose a place.
- When is high tide?
- When is low tide?
- How long is it between high and low tide?

- Is it the same every day? Why? Why not?

5d Symmetrical sea

- collection of sea shells
- pictures of sea creatures
- pencil and paper

- Investigate symmetry in sea shells.
- Draw the shells and show their lines of symmetry.

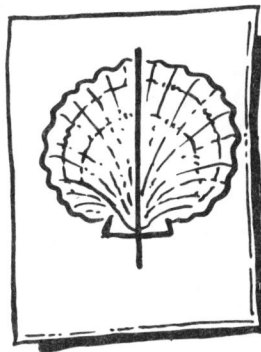

- What about symmetry in other sea creatures?
- Draw the creatures and show their lines of symmetry.

6a Jobs around the house

- pencil and paper

- What jobs need doing at home each day?
- Who does them?
- How long do they take?
- Make a chart of all the jobs that are done each day, how long they take and who does them.

- Now think about the jobs that need doing once a week and do the same as above.
- What about once a month?
- Compare your charts.

6b Jobs worth

- pencil and paper

- Make a list of all the jobs that need doing at home.
- Think about how much each job is worth.
- How much money would you get in a week if you were paid for all the jobs you do?
- What about other members of your family?

- How much money would you earn in a month / a year?
- What about other members of your family?

6c Cooking

- Work out how much of each ingredient you would need to make an omelette for:
  - 2 people
  - 5 people
  - 8 people
  - 14 people
  - everyone in your class.

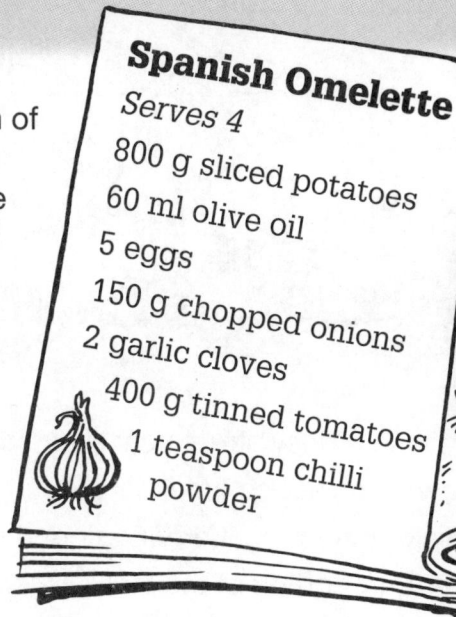

Spanish Omelette
Serves 4
800 g sliced potatoes
60 ml olive oil
5 eggs
150 g chopped onions
2 garlic cloves
400 g tinned tomatoes
1 teaspoon chilli powder

- recipe book
- pencil and paper

- Choose a recipe of your own and work out how much of each ingredient you would need to feed 5 people, 10 people, 12 people, everyone in your class.

6d Painting

AJAX PAINT
5 litres is enough to cover 50 m².

- measuring equipment
- pencil and paper

- Imagine you are painting the walls and ceiling of your living room.
- Work out the area of the walls and ceiling and calculate how many litres of paint you will need.

- What if you were going to paint the whole of the inside of your home? Estimate how many litres of paint you would need.

7a Street uses

- pencil and paper

- Choose a busy street near your school.
- How is the space on either side of the street used?
- Think about the different categories you can divide the street into.
- What proportion of the street is used for each of your categories?

- Compare this with another street, perhaps the street your school is on.

7b Street map

- squared paper
- ruler
- coloured pencils
- pencil and paper

- Using squared paper, draw a map of the area around your school.
- Mark on your map at least 10 different things in the area, e.g. the school, a shop, a post box, your house, a large tree…
- Label the columns: A, B, C, D, …
- Label the rows: 1, 2, 3, 4, …
- Now make a list of the different things on your map with their grid reference.

- Write directions so that someone can find their way from one place on your map to another.

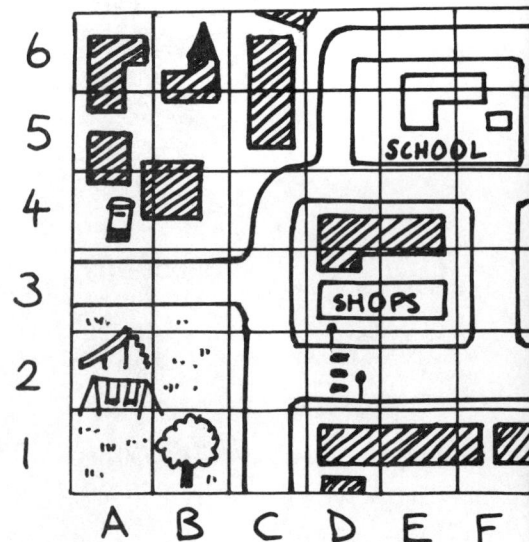

7c

People in your street

- pencil and paper

- Estimate how many people live in your street.
- Think about the number of houses / blocks of flats in your street.
- Think about how many people live in each house / flat.
- What proportion do you think are adults / children?

- How does this compare with the number of people who live in the street your school is on?

7d

Money trail

- measuring equipment
- one coin of each denomination
- pencil and paper

- Estimate then work out how many 10p coins you would need to stretch the length of the street your school is on. (If the street is too long, then what about the length of the block the school is on?)
- How much money would your trail be worth?

- What if you used only £1, £2, 50p, 20p or 5p coins instead? How many coins would you need?
- What different totals would you get if you had a trail of £1 coins, £2 coins, …?
- How does using different coins affect your answers?

8a School recycling

- measuring equipment
- pencil and paper

PAPER

- What things can you recycle?
- What things does your school recycle?
- How much of each thing do they recycle?
- What else could your school recycle?
  Find out how much they could recycle of each thing.

FOR COMPOST

CANS

- How are you going to measure each amount?

8b Home recycling

- measuring equipment
- pencil and paper

Card

Newspapers

Glass

charity shop stuff

Cans

- What things do you recycle at home?
- How much of each thing do you recycle?
- How could you encourage people to recycle more things in their homes?

- If the encouragement includes money, what would be a fair price for recycling different types of things?

8c Rubbish

• measuring equipment
• pencil and paper

- How much rubbish does your school produce that is not recycled?
- How are you going to measure this?

- Think about the bins in your school.
  - Where are they located?
  - How big are they?
  - How often are they emptied?

8d Second-hand stall

• pencil and paper

Class 4 Second-hand Stall

- Plan a class second-hand stall.
- What things do you have at home that you don't use any more?
- How much do you think someone else would pay for each of them?
- How much money would you raise if you sold them all?

- How much would the whole class raise?
- What would you do with the money?

9a Popular cars

• pencil and paper

- What is the most popular make of car in your area?
- Record your results in a graph.

- What is the most popular colour?

9b Family car

• pencil and paper

- How many miles does a family with one car travel in a week?
- How much petrol do they use?
- How much does this cost?

- Estimate the total number of miles travelled in a year, and how much this costs in petrol.

9c Number plates

- pencil and paper

- Write down the number from each of the number plates in your school car park.
- Using any three of these numbers, how close can you get to a total of 1000 using one or more of the four operations: $+ - \times \div$?

- What if you used any four of the numbers?

9d Travelling

- pencil and paper

The distance between London and Liverpool is 357 km.

Kilometre Chart	Birmingham	Cardiff	Liverpool	London
Birmingham		185	156	193
Cardiff	185		333	247
Liverpool	156	333		357
London	193	247	357	

- If you wanted to visit each of the four cities above by car, what is the shortest route you could take?
- How long is this route?

- If you were driving at 110 km an hour, how long would this take you?

10a Planning a holiday

- hotel brochures
- holiday section of newspaper
- pencil and paper

- Plan a holiday abroad for you and your family.
- Choose a place you would like to visit.
- Work out how much your holiday will cost.

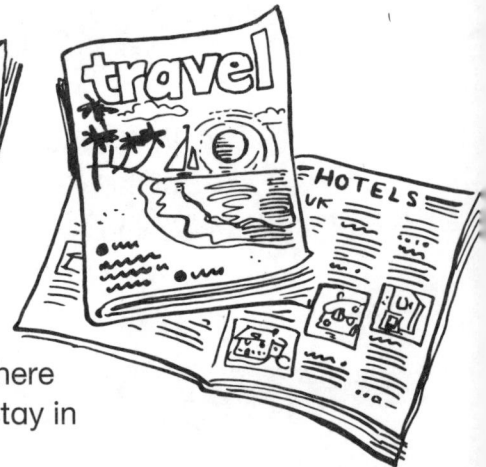

- Think about:
  - how long you will go for
  - how you will get there
  - how you will get around once you are there
  - what type of accommodation you will stay in
  - if you will take out travel insurance
  - if you will cook your own food or eat out
  - other expenses such as sightseeing and souvenirs.

10b Package holiday

- package holiday brochures
- pencil and paper

- Choose a package holiday for you and your family to go on.
- What will be the cost?
- What is included in this cost?
- What is not included? How much extra will this cost?

- How would the cost be affected if you went at a different time of the year? Why do you think this is?

10c Visiting our local area

- brochures of places of interest in the local area
- pencil and paper

- Imagine you work for the local tourist board.
- Plan an itinerary for a three day visit to your local area.

- What places of interest should you include?
- Approximately how long will it take people to get from one place to another?
- How long would you expect someone to spend at each place?
- Don't forget to allow time for them to eat and rest!

10d School holidays

- list of next year's school term dates
- ruler
- pencil and paper

- Draw a calendar for the next academic year.
- Mark which days are school days and which days are holidays.
- What proportion of the year do you spend on holidays?

- Don't forget to include bank holidays, half terms and the summer holidays at the end of the academic year.

11a

Newly designed classroom

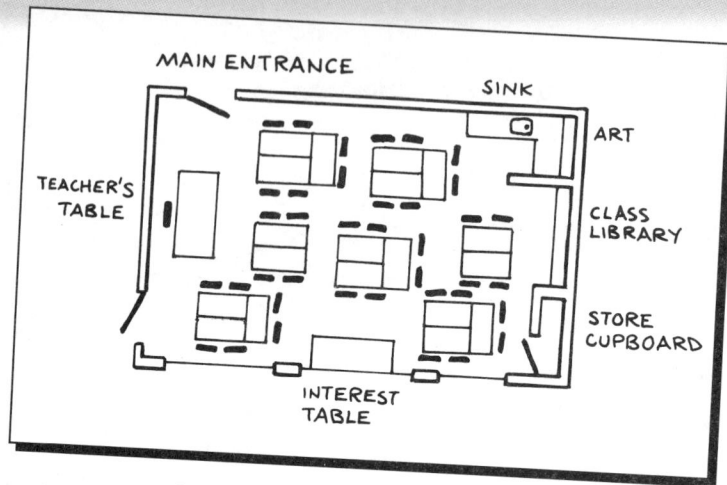

- squared paper
- ruler
- pencil and paper

MAIN ENTRANCE

SINK

ART

TEACHER'S TABLE

CLASS LIBRARY

STORE CUPBOARD

INTEREST TABLE

- Redesign your classroom.
- Draw a scale plan of your new classroom design.

- Everything that you see in your classroom should stay.
- Remember to leave enough space between the different types of furniture for everyone to move about.

11b

Paper

- pencil and paper

- How much paper does your class use in a week?

- How does this compare with other classes in your school?
- How much paper does your school use over a year?

11c Windows

- measuring equipment
- pencil and paper

- How many square metres of glass would be needed to replace all the windows in your classroom?

- Estimate how many square metres of glass would be needed to replace all the windows in your school.

11d How many children?

- measuring equipment
- pencil and paper

- Investigate how many children could fit into your classroom if all the children were standing and the classroom had no furniture in it.

- What if every child was sitting down crossed legged?

12a Shops in the local area

- pencil and paper

- Choose a shopping centre or High Street near you.
- How many shops are there?
- Group the shops.
- Why did you choose these groups?
- How else could you group them?

- Think about:
  - shop size
  - types of goods sold.

12b Biggest and busiest

- pencil and paper

- Choose a shopping centre or High Street near you.
- Which are the busiest shops?
- Which are the quietest shops?
- Do bigger shops have more customers than smaller shops?

- Does a certain type of shop have more customers than others?
- Why do you think this is?

12c Cost of the same item

- pencil and paper

- Investigate the cost of buying the same item in different shops.
- Is there much difference in the price? How much?
- Why do you think this is so?
- Do this for a number of different items.

- Is there a different way of buying any of these items than in a shop? How does the price compare?

12d Packaging

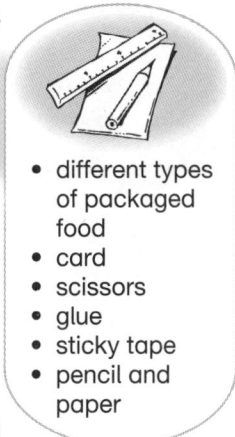

- different types of packaged food
- card
- scissors
- glue
- sticky tape
- pencil and paper

- Look at the way a variety of foods are packaged.
- Why do you think they are packaged in these shapes?
- Without opening the packing, construct one of these shapes out of card.

- Write instructions for someone else to be able to make your package.

13 Making numbers

- 1–9 digit cards
- pencil and paper

- Shuffle a set of 1–9 digit cards.
- Deal the top four cards and place them face up on the table.
- Use these digit cards to make 24 different 4-digit numbers.
- Order your numbers smallest to largest.
- Round each number to the nearest multiple of 10.
- Round each number to the nearest multiple of 100.

- What if you dealt five digit cards and used them to make 5-digit numbers?

---

14 Ordering numbers

- pencil and paper

| -6 | | -4 | | 0 | | 3 |

- Look at the cards above.
- Write numbers for each of the blank cards so that the seven numbers are in order.
- How many different ways can you think of?

- What if you had these numbers instead?

| -8 | | -5 | | -2 | | 2 |

15 Nearest 10 and 100

- pencil and paper

- Investigate which numbers are 650 when rounded to the nearest 10 and are 700 when rounded to the nearest 100.
- Which numbers are 4150 when rounded to the nearest 10 and 4100 when rounded to the nearest 100?

- What if the numbers are 6700 when rounded to the nearest 100 and 7000 when rounded to the nearest 1000?

16 Divisible by 4

- pencil and paper

If a number is divisible by 4, the last 2 digits of the number are divisible by 4.

- Is Rebecca right? Why? Why not?

If a number is divisible by 3, the sum of its digits is divisible by 3.

- Is Rebecca right this time? Why? Why not?

- Think of a rule for numbers divisible by 6.

17 Multiples of 10 between...

- pencil and paper

I'm thinking of a number between 5797 and 6011. It is a multiple of 10 but not a multiple of 100.

- Investigate what numbers it could be.

- What if the number was between 34 826 and 35 124?

18 Number sequences

- pencil and paper

3, 2, 1, 0, -1, -2

- Starting with –12 and ending with 12, what different whole number sequences can you make?
- You can only use each number from –12 to 12 once in each sequence and your sequence must have at least three numbers in it.
- Here is one: –12, –10, –8, –6, –4, –2, 0, 2, 4, 6, 8, 10, 12.

- What if you can use whole numbers and decimal numbers?
- What if you started at 20 and ended with –20?

19 Common multiples

• pencil and paper

2 times-table
2, 4, 6,
8, 12, 14,
16, 18

10, 20,
30, 40,
50

5 times-table
5, 15, 25,
35, 45

• Think about multiples in the 2, 3, 4, 5 and 10 times-tables.
• Use Venn diagrams to write about the multiples that occur in two of the above tables.
• Write about what you notice.

• What if you used Venn diagrams to write about the multiples that occur in three of the above tables?
• What about the multiples of 2, 3, 4, 5, 6, 7, 8, 9 and 10?

---

20 Rolling fractions

• 0–9 die
• pencil and paper

• Roll a 0–9 die twice.
• Use the numbers rolled to make a fraction. The first number rolled is the numerator, the second number is the denominator.
• Do this 20 times.
• Order the fractions smallest to largest.
• Which of the fractions are less than 1, greater than 1, equal to 1?
• Are there any equivalent fractions?

$$\frac{3}{4} \quad \frac{6}{9}$$
$$\frac{2}{7}$$
$$\frac{4}{1} \quad \frac{8}{9}$$

• What if the first number rolled was the denominator and the second number was the numerator?

21 Fractions of amounts

- 0–9 digit cards
- pencil and paper

- Choose four of the remaining digit cards to complete the fraction statement below.
- In each statement you can only use each digit card once.

$$\frac{1}{\Box} \times \Box\Box = \Box$$

0		2	3	4
	5	6	7	8	9

- What other different fraction statements can you make?

- What if you chose five digit cards to complete this fraction statement?

$$\frac{\Box}{\Box} \times \Box\Box = \Box$$

- What about using six digit cards?

$$\frac{\Box}{\Box} \times \Box\Box = \Box\Box$$

---

22 Fraction families

- calculator
- pencil and paper

- Investigate what happens when you convert fraction families, e.g. $\frac{1}{4}$, $\frac{2}{4}$, $\frac{3}{4}$, into decimals.
- Do this for quarters and tenths.
- What patterns do you notice?

- What happens if you continue the families into improper fractions, e.g. $\frac{4}{4}$, $\frac{5}{4}$, $\frac{6}{4}$...?
- What about fifths and eighths?

23 Making decimals

- 0–9 die
- pencil and paper

- Roll a 0–9 die three times.
- After each roll of the die write down the number.
- Use the three numbers rolled to make as many different decimal numbers as you can.
- Use decimal numbers with 1 and 2 decimal places.
- Order your numbers smallest to largest.
- Now round each decimal number to the nearest whole number.

- What if you used the three numbers rolled to make as many different whole numbers and decimal numbers as you can?

© HarperCollins*Publishers* Ltd 2005

---

24 2 numbers totalling 100

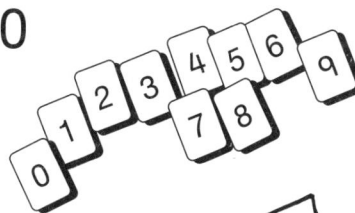

- 0–9 digit cards
- pencil and paper

$$\boxed{}\boxed{} + \boxed{}\boxed{} = 100$$

- Investigate different ways of completing this addition statement using any four digit cards.
- You can only use each digit card once in each calculation.
- How many different calculations can you make?

74 + 26
13 + 87

- What if you could use each digit more than once in each calculation?

© HarperCollins*Publishers* Ltd 2005

25 Consecutive decimals

- pencil and paper

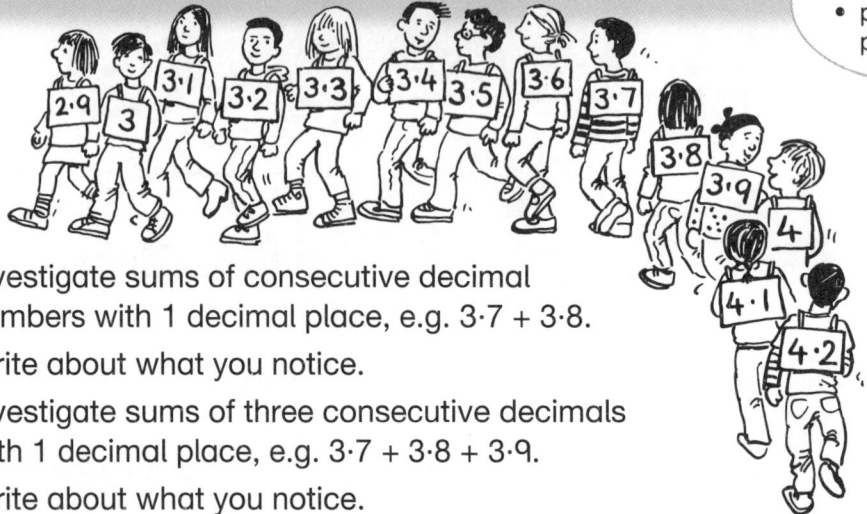

- Investigate sums of consecutive decimal numbers with 1 decimal place, e.g. 3·7 + 3·8.
- Write about what you notice.
- Investigate sums of three consecutive decimals with 1 decimal place, e.g. 3·7 + 3·8 + 3·9.
- Write about what you notice.

- What if you investigated sums of consecutive decimals with 2 decimal places, e.g. 3·57 + 3·58?
- What if you investigated sums of three consecutive decimals with 2 decimal places, e.g. 3·57 + 3·58 + 3·59?
- What if you investigated sums of four or five consecutive decimals?

---

26 Addition and subtraction cards

- 1–9 digit cards
- pencil and paper

$$\square\square + \square\square = \square\square$$

- Choose six digit cards to make complete addition calculations, including the answer.
- In each calculation you can only use each digit card once.
- Here is an example:

$$3\ 2 + 1\ 5 = 4\ 7$$

- Investigate how many different calculations you can make.

- What if you chose six digit cards to make complete subtraction calculations?

27 Totals and differences

- pencil and paper

- Write down any three digits from 1 to 9.
- Arrange the digits to make six different 2-digit numbers.
- Investigate different totals using three of the six numbers.
- How many different totals can you make?
- Write each of the different totals in order, smallest to largest, and find the difference between each successive total.
- Do you notice anything?

- What if you found the totals of four of the six numbers?

28 Dice calculations

- 1–6 die
- 0–9 die
- pencil and paper

- Roll a 1–6 die four times.
- After each roll of the die, write down the number so you don't forget it.
- Use the four numbers rolled to make 24 different 3-digit numbers.
- Which two of your numbers have:
  - the smallest total?
  - the smallest difference?
  - the largest total?
  - the largest difference?

6, 3, 1, 4

134	314	413	613
136	316	416	614
143	341	431	631
146	346	436	634
163	361	461	641
164	364	463	643

- What if you used a 0–9 die instead?

29 3-card calculations

- 1–9 digit cards
- pencil and paper

- Shuffle a set of 1–9 digit cards.
- Deal the top three cards and place them face up on the table.
- Use these digit cards to make as many different 2-digit and 3-digit numbers as you can.
- Choose any two of the numbers you have made and add them together.
- Choose any three of the numbers you have made and add them together.

- What if you chose three numbers then added two of the numbers together and subtracted the third?

© HarperCollins*Publishers* Ltd 2005

30 Making predictions

- pencil and paper

- Write down two 3-digit even numbers.
- If you were to add the two numbers together, would your answer be an odd or an even number?
- What if you were to find the difference between the two numbers? Would the answer be an odd or an even number?
- Estimate the answers to the addition and subtraction calculations.
- Calculate the answers.
- Were your predictions correct? Why? Why not?
- What happens when you write down two 3-digit odd numbers?
- What about one odd and one even 3-digit number?

386 + 657

- What if you chose three numbers to make an addition calculation?
- What if you chose three numbers then added two of the numbers together and subtracted the third?

© HarperCollins*Publishers* Ltd 2005

31 Consecutive reversals

- pencil and paper

- Write a 3-digit number using three consecutive digits.
- Reverse the digits and find the sum of the two numbers.
- How many different calculations can you make in this way?
- Write about any patterns you notice.

- What if you found the difference between these two numbers?
- What if you used three consecutive even digits or three consecutive odd digits?

© HarperCollins*Publishers* Ltd 2005

---

32 Reversing palindromic numbers

- pencil and paper

The digits in a palindromic number read the same backwards as forwards.

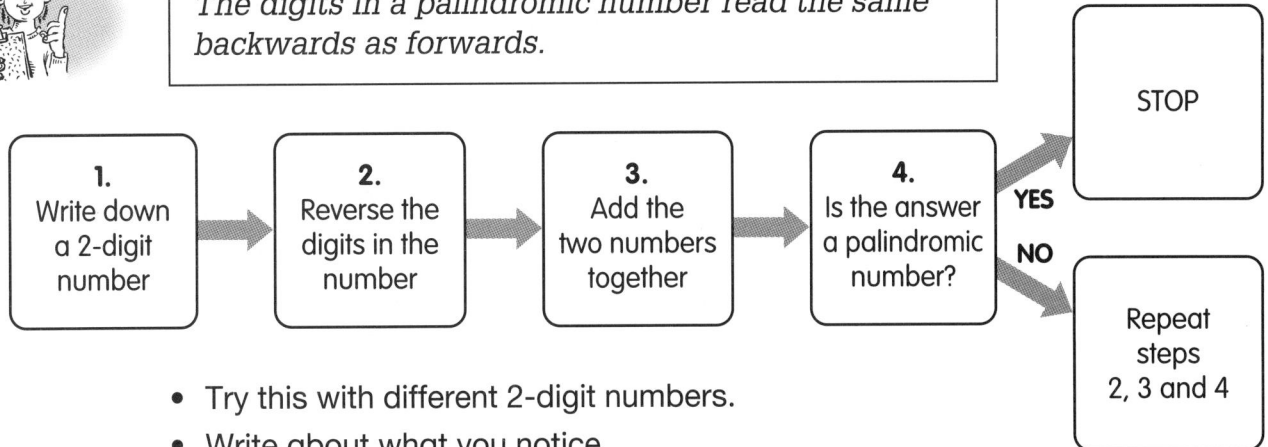

1. Write down a 2-digit number	2. Reverse the digits in the number	3. Add the two numbers together	4. Is the answer a palindromic number?	YES → STOP
				NO → Repeat steps 2, 3 and 4

- Try this with different 2-digit numbers.
- Write about what you notice.

- What happens if you find the difference between the two numbers?
- What if you used 3-digit numbers?

© HarperCollins*Publishers* Ltd 2005

33 Telephone totals

- pencil and paper

- Write down your telephone number.
- Separate the digits and find the total.
- Investigate separating the digits in other ways. Find the total each time.

- What if you separated the digits to make subtraction calculations? However, you must make sure that your answers are always positive numbers.

My telephone number
is 73174953
73+17+49+53 = 192
7+3+1+7+4+9+5+3 = 39
731+749+53 = 1533
7317+4953 = 12 270
7317+49+

---

34 Using tables

- pencil and paper

$1 \times 3 = 3$
$2 \times 3 = 6$
$3 \times 3 = 9$
$4 \times 3 = 12$
$5 \times$

- Write out the 3 times-table.
- Investigate how you can use the 3 times-table to help you with the 6 times-table.
- How does the 6 times-table help you with the 12 times-table?

- How can you use the 4 times-table to help work out the 8 times-table?
- What about the 10 times-table to help you with the 9 and 11 times-tables?

35 Multiplying by 19 and 21

- pencil and paper

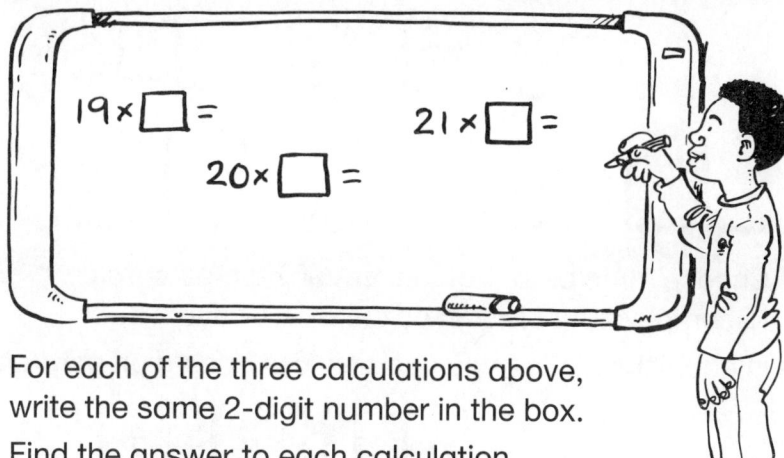

$$19 \times \square =$$

$$21 \times \square =$$

$$20 \times \square =$$

- For each of the three calculations above, write the same 2-digit number in the box.
- Find the answer to each calculation.
- Do this five times using a different 2-digit number each time.
- How did you work out the answers?

- What if the 3 numbers were 29, 30 and 31 instead of 19, 20 and 21?

36 2-digit x 1-digit

- 0–9 die
- pencil and paper

- Roll a 0–9 die three times and write down the numbers.
- Use the three numbers to make a 2-digit number and a 1-digit number.
- Multiply the two numbers together.
- By re-arranging the three numbers, investigate what other products you can make by multiplying a 2-digit number by a 1-digit number.
- What is the largest / smallest answer you can make?

- What if you rolled the die four times to make a 3-digit number and a 1-digit number?
- What if you used the three numbers rolled to make a 2-digit decimal number and a 1-digit number?

37 Division cards

- 0–9 digit cards
- pencil and paper

$$\boxed{0}\ \boxed{1}\ \boxed{2}\ \boxed{3}\ \boxed{4}\ \boxed{5}\ \ \ \boxed{7}\ \boxed{8}\ \boxed{9}$$

$$\boxed{}\boxed{} \div \boxed{6} = \boxed{} \quad \text{or} \quad \boxed{}\boxed{} \div \boxed{6} = \boxed{}\boxed{}$$

- Choose three or four of the remaining digit cards to complete the division calculation above.
- In each calculation you can only use each digit card once.
- Here is an example: $\boxed{4}\ \boxed{2} \div \boxed{6} = \boxed{7}$
- Investigate how many different calculations you can make.

- What if you replaced the '6' digit card with the '7', '8' or '9' digit card?

---

38 Dividing by 7

- pencil and paper

- Write down any 2-digit number.
- Divide your number by 7.
- What is the remainder?
- Write down other 2-digit numbers and divide them by 7.
- What do you notice about all the remainders?

- What if you divided each of your numbers by 6?

39

9

70

34

481

773

8

1

300

25

2

13

- pencil and paper

- Investigate making as many division calculations as you can with the answer 9.

- What about with an answer of 9 r 2?

---

40 Many multiplications

- pencil and paper

- Using only the unbroken keys on this calculator, how many different products can you make pressing four or more of the keys? You can press each key only once in each calculation.

- What if the ⊠ was broken and instead you used the ➗?

41 Broken calculator

- calculator
- pencil and paper

- Using only the unbroken keys on this calculator, make the following totals.

  99   270   616   72
  135   36   0   29

- You can use each key more than once in each calculation.

- Can you find more than one way?

- What if you used this calculator instead?

---

42 True statements

- pencil and paper

$$4 + \square < 2 \times \triangle$$

$$24 \div \square < 24 - \triangle$$

- Write as many different solutions as you can for the missing numbers.

- What if you changed the < sign to a > sign?

43

1, 10, 100 and 1000

- pencil and paper

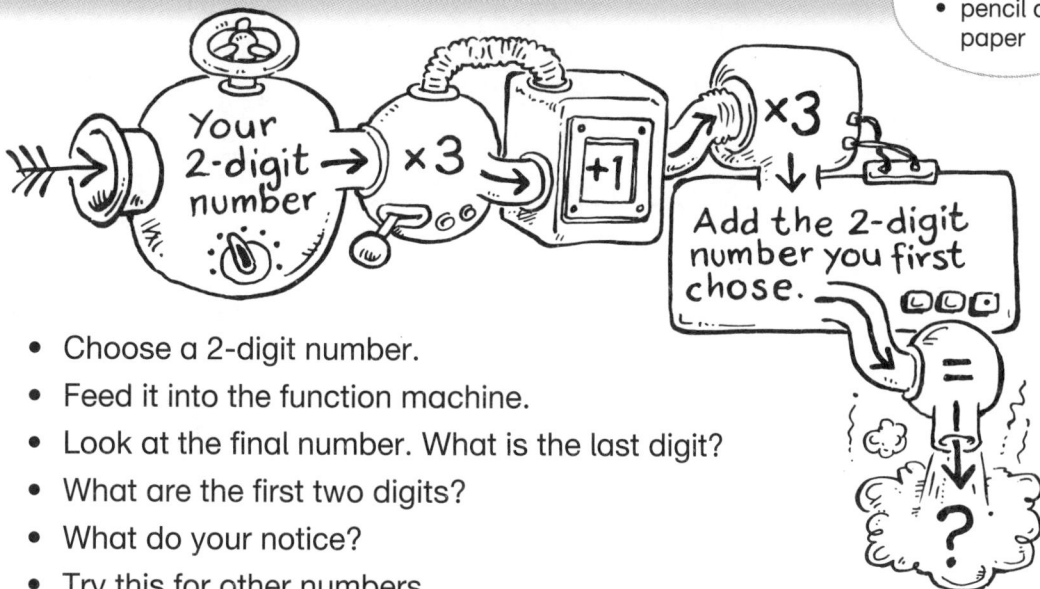

- Write down any 4-digit number.
- In each of the calculations below write the 4-digit number in the box.

| $\boxed{} + 10$ | $\boxed{} + 100$ | $\boxed{} + 1000$ | $\boxed{} + 1$ |

| $\boxed{} - 100$ | $\boxed{} - 1000$ | $\boxed{} - 1$ | $\boxed{} - 10$ |

- Work out the answers.
- Choose another 4-digit number and do the same thing.
- What do you notice about your answers for each different 4-digit number you chose?
- What happens when you use a 3-digit number instead of a 4-digit number?

- What if the calculations were these?

| $\boxed{} \times 1$ | $\boxed{} \times 10$ | $\boxed{} \times 100$ |

| $\boxed{} \div 100$ | $\boxed{} \div 10$ | $\boxed{} \div 1$ |

44

Amazing function machines

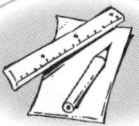

- pencil and paper

Your 2-digit number → ×3 → +1 → ×3 → Add the 2-digit number you first chose. → ?

- Choose a 2-digit number.
- Feed it into the function machine.
- Look at the final number. What is the last digit?
- What are the first two digits?
- What do your notice?
- Try this for other numbers.

- Make your own amazing function machine. What amazing things can you make it do? Give it to a friend to use.

45 Domino calculations

- set of dominoes
- pencil and paper

- Choose any two dominoes and arrange them like this:
- Investigate possible domino addition calculations.

$$+ \quad \begin{array}{r} 63 \\ +45 \\ \hline 108 \end{array}$$

- Investigate possible domino subtraction calculations.

$$- \quad \begin{array}{r} 63 \\ -45 \\ \hline 18 \end{array}$$

- What about multiplication and division calculations?

$$\times \quad 54 \times 3 = 162 \qquad \div \quad 54 \div 3 = 18$$

46 £3 please!

- pencil and paper

There are six different ways of making £3 using only £2, £1 and 50p coins.

- Is Olivia right?

- What if you could use 20p and 10p coins as well?
- What about different ways of making £2.75?

47 Paying bills

• pencil and paper

• You only have one each of the following notes and coins.

• How would you pay bills involving whole numbers of pounds between £1 and £20? Offer as near to the amount of the bill as possible.

• What change would you receive for each of these amounts?

• What if you had one each of the following notes and coins? What bills could you pay involving a whole number of pounds between £1 and £40?

© HarperCollins*Publishers* Ltd 2005

---

48 Calculating with pence

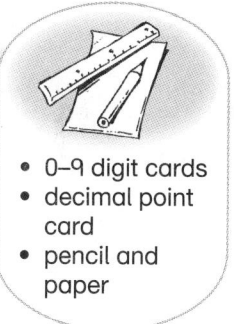

• 0–9 digit cards
• decimal point card
• pencil and paper

• Place the '0' digit card on the table with the decimal point card to the right of it.

`0` `·`

• Shuffle the remaining cards and deal the top three.

• Choose two of the cards and place them to the right of the decimal point to make a decimal number with tenths and hundredths.

`0` `·` `7` `3`

• Write this decimal with a pound sign to the left of the '0' card.

• How many different decimal numbers with tenths and hundredths can you make with the 3 cards you have dealt? Write them as amounts of money.

• Choose two of the amounts you have made and find the total.

• What other totals can you make using two of the amounts?

• What is the largest / smallest amount you can make?

• Find the difference between two of the amounts.

© HarperCollins*Publishers* Ltd 2005

49 Pounds and pence

- 0–9 die
- pencil and paper

- Roll a 0–9 die three times and write down the numbers.
- Use the three numbers to make six different pounds and pence amounts.
- Choose two of the amounts and find their total.
- What other totals can you make using two of the amounts?
- What is the largest / smallest amount you can make?

£6·89
£6·98
£8·69
£8·96
£9·68
£9·86

- What if you found the difference between two of the amounts?

50 Spirals

- squared paper
- ruler
- pencil and paper

- Copy this spiral onto squared paper.
- Continue the spiral as far as you can.
- Write about the total length of each line.
- What do you notice?
- What predictions can you make?

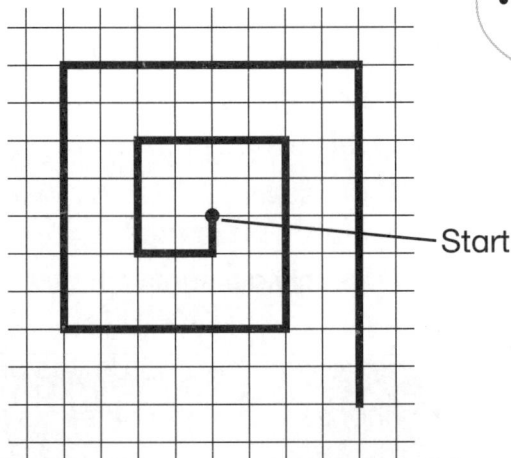

Start

- Make a different spiral. Give it to a friend to continue.

51 Shopping basket

• pencil and paper

• Investigate the different total masses you could have in your shopping basket if you only bought three of the following items.

• Which baskets weigh more than 1 kg? How much more?
• Which baskets weigh less than 1 kg? How much less?

• What if you bought four items?
• What about five items?

---

52 Making fruit juice

• pencil and paper

• Make a drink using two different types of fruit juices. Choose which two fruits you think will taste good together.
• Make the drink so that it is 0·3 of one juice and 0·7 of the other.
• How many millilitres of each juice do you need to fill a small glass?
• What about a medium glass?
• What about a large glass?

Small
200 ml

Medium
300 ml

Large
500 ml

• Now do the same thing using three different types of juice.
• Make the drink so that it is $\frac{1}{5}$ of the first juice, $\frac{3}{10}$ of the second juice and $\frac{1}{2}$ of the third juice.

• What if you made a drink using four different flavours of juice, one part in 20 of the first juice, 1 part in 4 of the second juice, 3 parts in 10 of the third juice and 2 parts in 5 of the fourth juice?

53 Light bars

- pencil and paper

> The display on a digital clock uses light bars to create digits. All the digits 0 to 9 can be made using up to seven light bars.

- Make all the digits 0 to 9 using the light bars.
- Write the following times as they would appear on a 12-hour digital clock:
  - when you wake up in the morning
  - the time school starts
  - the time it is now
  - when you have lunch
  - the time school finishes
  - when you go to bed.

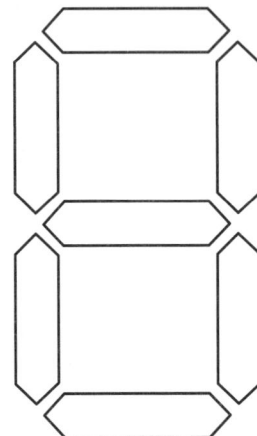

- What if you wrote the times as they would appear on a 24-hour digital clock?

54 Area and perimeter

- 1–6 die
- 1 cm squared paper
- ruler
- pencil and paper

- Roll a 1–6 die twice.
- Multiply together the two numbers rolled.
- Make a shape of this area.
- Can you make other shapes with the same area?

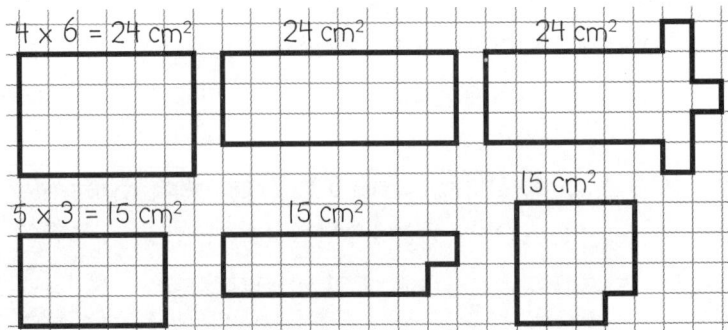

$4 \times 6 = 24$ cm²   24 cm²   24 cm²

$5 \times 3 = 15$ cm²   15 cm²   15 cm²

- What is the perimeter of each of your shapes?

55

Different areas and perimeters

- squared paper
- ruler
- pencil and paper

- Investigate drawing shapes that have areas of 12 cm² but different perimeters.

- Investigate drawing shapes that have perimeters of 12 cm but different areas.

56

Pentominoes

- squared paper
- pencil and paper

This is a pentomino. A pentomino is made by joining five squares, edge to edge.

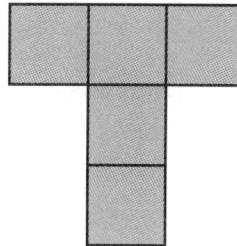

- How many different pentominoes can you make?

- How many of these pentominoes make an open cube?
- What if you joined the five squares corner to corner at right angles? How many different shapes could you make?

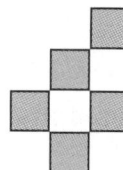

57 Symmetrical shapes

- about 30 Centicubes
- 1 cm squared paper
- pencil and paper

- Place 10 Centicubes to the left of the line on the grid below to make a shape.
- Use another 10 cubes to show the reflection of the shape in the mirror line.

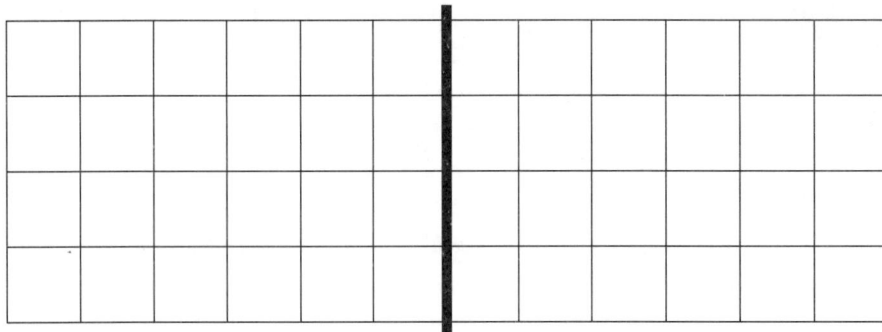

- Record your shapes.
- Make different shapes with between 10 and 15 Centicubes. Ask a friend to show the reflection of the shape in the mirror line.

- What if the mirror line was horizontal?

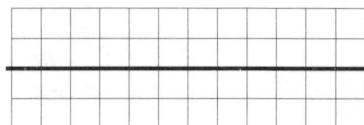

58 Shortest route

- pencil and paper

One of the shortest routes from Point A to Point C is (3, 6), (3, 5), (3, 4), (3, 3), (3, 2) and (4, 2). It is a total distance of 6 units.

- What other routes can you take from Point A to Point C in 6 units?
- What is the shortest route to travel from Point A to Point B? Is there more than one way?
- What about the shortest route from Point A to Point D? Is there more than one way?

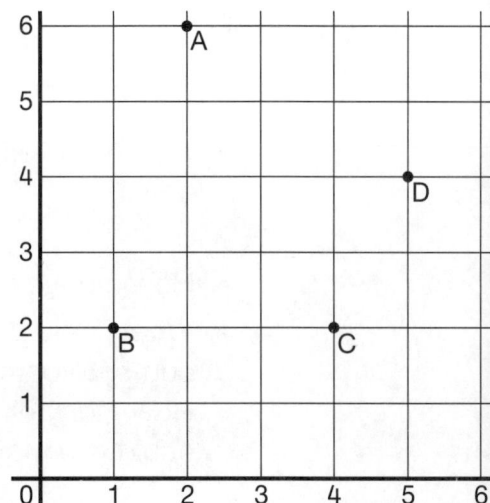

- Investigate the shortest routes from Point B to Points C and D.
- What about the shortest route from Point C to Point D?

59 Right angles?

- squared paper
- ruler
- pencil and paper

- Draw the following shapes:
  - square
  - right angle triangle
  - isosceles triangles
  - regular octagon
  - regular hexagon
  - rectangle
  - equilateral triangle
  - regular pentagon
  - regular heptagon

- On each shape, mark the angles that are:
  - less than a right angle
  - right angles
  - more than a right angle.

- Write about what you notice.

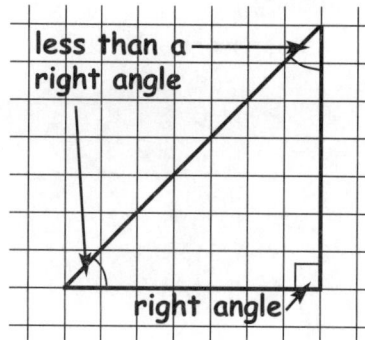

- What if you drew irregular shapes like these?

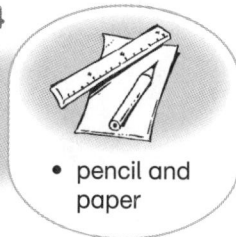

---

60 Angle times

- pencil and paper

An angle that is less than a right angle is called an 'acute angle'.
An angle that is greater than a right angle is called an 'obtuse angle'.

- Investigate for which o'clock times the angle between the minute and hour hands is:
  - an acute angle
  - a right angle
  - an obtuse angle.

- What about the angles between the minute and hour hands as they move between 4 o'clock and 5 o'clock?

Answers

Activity 14

The numbers can be ordered in 6 different ways:

−6, −5, −4, −3, 0, 1, 3
−6, −5, −4, −3, 0, 2, 3
−6, −5, −4, −2, 0, 1, 3
−6, −5, −4, −2, 0, 2, 3
−6, −5, −4, −1, 0, 1, 3
−6, −5, −4, −1, 0, 2, 3

Activity 15

Numbers that are 650 when rounded to the nearest 10 and 700 when rounded to the nearest 100 are: 650, 651, 652, 653 and 654.

Numbers that are 4150 when rounded to the nearest 10 and 4100 when rounded to the nearest 100 are: 4145, 4146, 4147, 4148 and 4149.

Activity 16

Rebecca is right. If a number is divisible by 4, the last 2 digits of the number are divisible by 4 and if a number is divisible by 3, the sum of its digits are divisible by 3.

Activity 17

5810, 5820, 5830, 5840, 5850, 5860, 5870, 5880, 5890, 5910, 5920, 5930, 5940, 5950, 5960, 5970, 5980, 5990, 6010

Activity 18

−12, −11, −10, −9, −8, −7, −6, −5, −4, −3, −2, −1, 0, 1, 2, 3, 4, 5, 6, 7, 8, 9, 10, 11, 12
−12, −10, −8, −6, −4, −2, 0, 2, 4, 6, 8, 10, 12
−12, −9, −6, −3, 0, 3, 6, 9, 12
−12, −8, −4, 0, 4, 8, 12
−12, −6, 0, 6, 12
−12, −4, 4, 12
−12, 0, 12

Activity 19

- The following numbers are multiples of 2 and multiples of 3: 6, 12 and 18. They are also all multiples of 6.
- The following numbers are multiples of 2 and multiples of 4: 4, 8, 12, 16 and 20.
- The following numbers are multiples of 2 and multiples of 5: 10 and 20. They are also all multiples of 10.
- The following numbers are multiples of 2 and multiples of 10: 10 and 20.
- The following numbers are multiples of 3 and multiples of 4: 12, 24 and 36. They are also all multiples of 12.
- The following numbers are multiples of 3 and multiples of 5: 15 and 30. They are also all multiples of 15.
- The following number is a multiple of 3 and multiple of 10: 30. It is also a multiple of 30.
- The following numbers are multiples of 4 and multiples of 5: 20 and 40. They are also all multiples of 20.
- The following numbers are multiples of 4 and multiples of 10: 20 and 40. They are also all multiples of 20.
- The following numbers are multiples of 5 and multiples of 10: 10, 20, 30, 40 and 50.

Activity 21

30 different fraction statements are possible.

$\frac{1}{2} \times 06 = 3$ $\frac{1}{4} \times 08 = 2$

$\frac{1}{2} \times 08 = 4$ $\frac{1}{4} \times 20 = 5$

$\frac{1}{3} \times 06 = 2$ $\frac{1}{4} \times 28 = 7$

$\frac{1}{3} \times 24 = 8$ $\frac{1}{4} \times 32 = 8$

$\frac{1}{3} \times 27 = 9$ $\frac{1}{4} \times 36 = 9$

$\frac{1}{5} \times 20 = 4$ $\frac{1}{8} \times 24 = 3$

$\frac{1}{5} \times 30 = 6$ $\frac{1}{8} \times 32 = 4$

$\frac{1}{5} \times 40 = 8$ $\frac{1}{8} \times 40 = 5$

$\frac{1}{6} \times 30 = 5$ $\frac{1}{8} \times 56 = 7$

$\frac{1}{6} \times 42 = 7$ $\frac{1}{8} \times 72 = 9$

$\frac{1}{6} \times 54 = 9$ $\frac{1}{9} \times 27 = 3$

$\frac{1}{7} \times 28 = 4$ $\frac{1}{9} \times 36 = 4$

$\frac{1}{7} \times 42 = 6$ $\frac{1}{9} \times 54 = 6$

$\frac{1}{7} \times 56 = 8$ $\frac{1}{9} \times 63 = 7$

$\frac{1}{7} \times 63 = 9$ $\frac{1}{9} \times 72 = 8$

Activity 22

- $\frac{1}{4}, \frac{2}{4}, \frac{3}{4} = 0.25, 0.5, 0.75$
  Just as each fraction increases by one quarter, so too each decimal increases by one quarter, or 0.25

- $\frac{1}{10}, \frac{2}{10}, \frac{3}{10}, \frac{4}{10}, \frac{5}{10}, \frac{6}{10}, \frac{7}{10}, \frac{8}{10}, \frac{9}{10}$
  = 0.1, 0.2, 0.3, 0.4, 0.5, 0.6, 0.7, 0.8, 0.9
  Just as each fraction increases by one tenth, so too each decimal increases by one tenth, or 0.1

Activity 24

You can make 24 different calculations that total 100 involving pairs of 2-digit numbers where each of the digits in the 2-digit numbers is different.

21 + 79	03 + 97
31 + 69	13 + 87
41 + 59	43 + 57
51 + 49	53 + 47
61 + 39	83 + 17
71 + 29	93 + 07
02 + 98	04 + 96
32 + 68	14 + 86
42 + 58	24 + 76
52 + 48	74 + 26
62 + 38	84 + 16
92 + 08	94 + 06

Activity 25

- Sums of consecutive decimal numbers with 1 decimal place, e.g. 3·7 + 3·8, can be calculated easily by doubling the first number and adding 0·1 (or doubling the second number and subtracting 0·1). The tenths digit is always an odd number.
- Sums of three consecutive decimals with 1 decimal place, e.g. 3·7 + 3·8 + 3·9, can be calculated easily by multiplying the middle number by 3.

Activity 26

Accept any calculations of a pair of 2-digit numbers where all the digits in the calculation, including the answer, are different, e.g. 32 + 15 = 47; 73 + 25 = 98

Activity 30

When pairs of even and/or odd numbers are added or subtracted, the following answers always apply:

E + E = E
E – E = E
O + O = E
O – O = E
O + E = O / E + O = O
O – E = O / E – O = O

Activity 31

7 different calculations can be made:

123 + 321 = 444
234 + 432 = 666
345 + 543 = 888
456 + 654 = 1110
567 + 765 = 1332
678 + 876 = 1554
789 + 987 = 1776

Accept any patterns that the children notice about the calculations and their answers, e.g. for each calculation the hundreds digit is the same as the tens digit.

Activity 32

When both digits in the number are added together, e.g. 34 = 3 + 4 = 7, (or 43 = 4 + 3 = 7) and the total is:

- less than 10: a palindromic number is produced in 1 step
- 11: a palindromic number is produced in 1 step
- 10, 12, or 13: a palindromic number is produced in 2 steps
- 14: a palindromic number is produced in 3 steps
- 15: a palindromic number is produced in 4 steps
- 16: a palindromic number is produced in 6 steps
- 17: a palindromic number is produced in 12 steps.
- 18: a palindromic number is produced in 5 steps.

Activity 34

You get the 6 times-table by doubling the answers to the 3 times-table.

You get the 12 times-table by doubling the answers to the 6 times-table.

Activity 35

To multiply a number by 19, multiply the number by 20 and subtract the number you are multiplying.

To multiply a number by 21, multiply the number by 20 and add the number you are multiplying.

Activity 37

18 ÷ 6 = 3	54 ÷ 6 = 9
30 ÷ 6 = 5	78 ÷ 6 = 13
42 ÷ 6 = 7	90 ÷ 6 = 15

Activity 38

All 2-digit numbers that are multiples of 7 have no remainders. All other numbers have remainders that are less than 7.

Activity 39

Accept any division calculations with an answer of 9, e.g.

18 ÷ 2
27 ÷ 3
90 ÷ 10
117 ÷ 13

Activity 40

65 different products can be made. (*168 appears twice as a product: 28 × 6 and 84 × 2.)

2 × 4 = 8	426 × 8 = 3408
2 × 6 = 12	428 × 6 = 2568
2 × 8 = 16	462 × 8 = 3696
4 × 6 = 24	468 × 2 = 936
4 × 8 = 32	482 × 6 = 2892
6 × 8 = 48	486 × 2 = 972
24 × 6 = 144	624 × 8 = 4992
24 × 8 = 192	628 × 4 = 2512
26 × 4 = 104	642 × 8 = 5136
26 × 8 = 208	648 × 2 = 1296
28 × 4 = 112	682 × 4 = 2728
28 × 6 = 168 *	684 × 2 = 1368
42 × 6 = 252	824 × 6 = 4944
42 × 8 = 336	826 × 4 = 3304
46 × 2 = 92	842 × 6 = 5052
46 × 8 = 368	846 × 2 = 1692
48 × 2 = 96	862 × 4 = 3448
48 × 6 = 288	864 × 2 = 1728
62 × 4 = 248	24 × 68 = 1632
62 × 8 = 496	24 × 86 = 2064
64 × 2 = 128	26 × 48 = 1248
64 × 8 = 512	26 × 84 = 2184
68 × 2 = 136	28 × 46 = 1288
68 × 4 = 272	28 × 64 = 1792
	42 × 68 = 2856
82 × 4 = 328	42 × 86 = 3612
82 × 6 = 492	62 × 48 = 2976
84 × 2 = 168 *	62 × 84 = 5208
84 × 6 = 504	82 × 46 = 3772
86 × 2 = 172	82 × 64 = 5248
86 × 4 = 344	

246 × 8 = 1968
248 × 6 = 1488
264 × 8 = 2112
268 × 4 = 1072
284 × 6 = 1704
286 × 4 = 1144

Answers

Activity 41

99 = 26 + 73
270 = 263 + 7
616 = 623 – 7
72 = 36 + 36
135 = 63 + 72
36 = 72 – 36
0 = 7 + 2 – 6 – 3
29 = 36 – 7
Other calculations are possible.

Activity 42

Many answers are possible, e.g.

4 + 1 < 2 × 3
or 4 + 2 < 2 × 4

24 ÷ 4 < 24 – 9
or 24 ÷ 2 < 24 – 2

Activity 44

All answers that come from the function machine have 3 as the units digit. Also, of the original 2-digit number that was chosen, the tens digit is now the hundreds digit and units digit is now the tens digit.

Activity 46

Olivia is right.
£2 + £1
£2 + 50p + 50p
£1 + £1 + £1
£1 + £1 + 50p + 50p
£1 + 50p + 50p + 50p + 50p
50p + 50p + 50p + 50p + 50p + 50p

Activity 47

£1 = £1 (no change)
£2 = £2 (no change)
£3 = £2 + £1 (no change)
£4 = £5 (£1 change)
£5 = £5 (no change)
£6 = £5 + £1 (no change)

£7 = £5 + £2 (no change)
£8 = £5 + £2 + £1 (no change)
£9 = £10 (£1 change)
£10 = £10 (no change)
£11 = £10 + £1 (no change)
£12 = £10 + £2 (no change)
£13 = £10 + £2 + £1 (no change)
£14 = £10 + £5 (£1 change)
£15 = £10 + £5 (no change)
£16 = £10 + £5 + £1 (no change)
£17 = £10 + £5 + £2 (no change)
£18 = £10 + £5 + £2 + £1 (no change)
£19 = Not enough money to pay the bill.
£20 = Not enough money to pay the bill.

Activity 50

The length of each new line increases by 1 square from the previous line.

Activity 52

For a fruit drink containing two different types of fruit juices:
Small: 60 ml of one juice and 140 ml of the other
Medium: 90 ml of one juice and 210 ml of the other
Large: 150 ml of one juice and 350 ml of the other

For a fruit drink containing three different types of fruit juices:
Small: 40 ml of the first juice, 60 ml of the second juice and 100 ml of the third
Medium: 60 ml of the first juice, 90 ml of the second juice and 150 ml of the third
Large: 100 ml of the first juice, 150 ml of the second juice and 250 ml of the third

Activity 56

There are 12 different pentominoes.

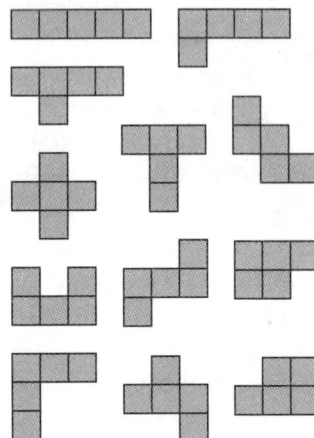

Activity 58

Another route from Point A to Point C in 6 units is (2, 5), (2, 4), (2, 3), (2, 2), (3, 2) and (4, 2).

The shortest possible route from Point A to Point B is in 5 units: (1, 6), (1, 5), (1, 4), (1, 3) and (1, 2) or (2, 5), (2, 4), (2, 3), (2, 2) and (1, 2).

The shortest possible route from Point A to Point D is in 5 units: (3, 6), (4, 6), (5, 6), (5, 5) and (5, 4) or (2, 5), (2, 4), (3, 4), (4, 4) and (5, 4).

Activity 60

The hands of the clock are at an acute angle at 1 o'clock, 2 o'clock, 10 o'clock and 11 o'clock.

The hands of the clock are at a right angle at 3 o'clock and 9 o'clock.

The hands of the clock are at an obtuse angle at 4 o'clock, 5 o'clock, 7 o'clock and 8 o'clock.